OH, HOW HE LOVES ME

REFLECTIONS OF GOD'S LOVE FOR ME AND FOR YOU

TINA A. HOBSON

International Best Selling Author

Heart Centered Women Publishing

A Division of Charlotte Howard

108 Flintlock Lane

Summerville, SC/USA 29483

www.HeartCenteredWomenPublishing.com

charlotte@thehairartistassociation.org

Book Cover ©2015 Heart Centered Women Publishing

Book Layout ©2015 Heart Centered Women Publishing

Ordering Information:

Quantity sales. Special discounts are available on quantity purchases by corporations, associations, and others. For details, contact the "Special Sales Department" at the address above.

Oh How He Loves Me: Reflections of God's Love For Me And For You. —1st ed.

ISBN-13: 978-0692409077

ASIN: 0692409076

Dedication

I dedicate this book to the three men who have been the best earthly fathers a girl could ever have. I thank my Heavenly Father for allowing you to be a part of my life. Oh, How He Loves Me.

Crawford Strickland; Uncle, I hardly ever showed my appreciation and love for you as I was so self absorbed, selfish and self centered. I was too busy seeking to know who my biological father was that I missed the opportunity to bask in the love you showed me every single day that you raised me. Oh, how you loved me.

James Adams Sr. Our start was a rocky one. Arguments and disagreements were many. I just knew that you didn't like me, therefore, how could you have loved me. Little did I know that behind every argument and disagreement was caring. I couldn't see it early on as I was too enthralled in alcohol and drug addiction. Once I became free of those demons I began to see clearly that you care. Being a man of few words, you don't always say that you care but you surely show it. Oh, how you love me.

James S. Edwards Sr., Another man of few words. Words could never have shown what a big heart you had. Your actions always showed how much you cared. You were the perfect example of how a man should care for a woman. You loved your family with the love of God. You gave me so many gifts that you were not aware of. You accepted me when few others would. Not one drop of blood made us relatives but you were still Daddy. The greatest gift you gave me was when I read the Bible, prayed and held your hand when you transitioned from earth to heaven. You showed me true beauty. Oh, how you loved me.

Foreword

One night I dreamed I was walking along the beach with the Lord.
Many scenes from my life flashed across the sky.
In each scene I noticed footprints in the sand.
Sometimes there were two sets of footprints,
other times there were one set of footprints.

This bothered me because I noticed
that during the low periods of my life,
when I was suffering from
anguish, sorrow or defeat,
I could see only one set of footprints.

So I said to the Lord,
"You promised me Lord,
that if I followed you,
you would walk with me always.
But I have noticed that during
the most trying periods of my life
there have only been one
set of footprints in the sand.
Why, when I needed you most,
you have not been there for me?"

The Lord replied,
"The times when you have
seen only one set of footprints,
is when I carried you."

The Lord carries us. It's never when we ask him to. It's not when we pray for him to intervening. Most folks talk to God the moment that things get rough. We have a tendency to call on him when the world becomes too much for us to handle. Most times we feel that the Lord is not listening. We wonder what am I doing wrong? Why have you not moved your hand? As with all things, the same situation that the Lord led us into is the same situation that he will get us out of. The Lord doesn't come when we ask. He is there before we part our lips to ask.

I started this foreword with the poem footprints for a reason. Footprints are the perfect example of the way God works. We do not need to ask the Lord to carry us. The only thing we have to do is to wait, believe, and be steadfast and ever ready. When the time is right, we will feel the hand of God move.

When I was a teenager, tribulations would enter my life. Like most problems they seemed from personal challenges I needed to solve; my family issues, my self-esteem issues, my faith issues, my confidence issues, not knowing how my bills would be paid after being diagnosed with carpal tunnel syndrome issues etc. I used to ask God why?

Why are these things happening to me? Why now Lord? Then I started to realize, that when these things happened, I would ALWAYS have the money and resources to take care of the problem. I stopped asking God why and started thanking him because he gave me a way to deal with the personal challenges I was facing in my life.

Then I started to ask the Lord to help me understand why these things would happen. I asked the Lord for clarity. I asked for understanding. This is what we need to ask the Lord for. This is what we need to understand. There will be trials in your life. There will be tribulations.

When these things happen, we need you to ask the Lord, what is the lesson? What are you teaching me? What do you want me to see Lord? I now ask God to give me the insight on what he is trying to show me.

Psalms 32:8 (KJV)
I will instruct thee and teach thee in the way which thou shalt go: I will guide thee with mine eye.

I am truly blessed and humbled to write the foreword of my beautiful sister Tina A. Hobson's book. Please share this book with your loved ones, friends and colleagues that are in need of a breakthrough in their lives.

With love,

Charlotte Howard
Women Life Mentor, 46X'S International Best Selling Publisher and Author
www.HeartCenteredWomenPublishing.com

ABOUT OH HOW HE LOVES ME,

REFLECTIONS OF GOD'S LOVE ME AND FOR YOU

This book is a 31 Day Devotional of how God loves me, understands me, has rescued me, and sustains me.

The Bible is full of scriptures that show God's love for me and for you. His love is everlasting and it never fails. As you read this book, my hope is that you can see that no matter what your circumstance may be or how much you and I may sin, God's love is always present and ready to make us better persons, if only we acknowledge and follow His voice and his loving commands.

I have added space at the end of each day's reflection for you to write your own reflections.

My personal reflections in this book are not in any type of chronological order of events as they occurred in my life. My brain does not always work like that. Nor are these all of God's evidence of how much he loves me. However, they are all true, coming from the heart, and given to me as God desired. I am more than sure that additional *reflections will be revealed to me in the future and as they are given to me I will pass them on to you.*

My prayer is that these pages will speak to you bringing you hope and peace, reminding you of how much God loves you.

"Above all, never lose *faith* in your FATHER IN HEAVEN who *loves you* more than you can comprehend."

~ Jeffrey R Holland

Before I *formed* you in the womb
I *knew* you,
before you were born
I *set you apart*.
Jeremiah 1:5

Reflection 1

Jeremiah 1:5- "Before I formed you in the womb I knew you and before you were born I consecrated you; I have appointed you a prophet to the nations."

What a precious gift that God gave us, the gift of life.

When I think about the goodness of The Lord, my heart sings Hallelujah. No other in the universe has ever or could ever give me the gift of life. Yes, birthed out of the womb of a woman but created by my heavenly Father.

I struggled for years due to not knowing who my earthly father was. Left feeling abandoned, unloved, misunderstood and incomplete. I would wonder who I really was, who I really looked like, where did my traits and characteristics come from.

One day during my struggle I was telling a friend about my feelings. That friend brought it to my attention that I did have a Father. My response was, "Oh no I don't, not now, not ever." I went on to tell them more of my feelings of discomfort by not knowing who I was. That friend shook their head and actually pointed their finger at me and said, "Who do you think created you?" They asked me if I believed in God, and I said "Yes, I do believe." They went on to explain to me how God loved and knew me before I was formed in the womb Jeremiah 1:5 "Before I formed you in the womb I knew you, And before you were born I consecrated you; I have appointed you a prophet to the nations."

I thought long and hard about what had been said to me. Yes, I did believe or did I? They say actions speak louder than words and I have to admit that what transpired in my life for years and years was no demonstration of believing in anything other than self. The journey to truly believe how much God loves me begins.

PERSONAL REFLECTION:

_____

_____

_____

_____

_____

_____

_____

_____

_____

_____

_____

_____

_____

I loved you at your darkest
Romans 5:8

Reflection 2

Romans 5:8 - But God demonstrates His own love toward us, in that while we were yet sinners, Christ died for us.

It's no secret (I'm Free and TGIF: Thank God I'm Forgiven) that many years of my life was lived in the troughs of alcohol and drug addiction. Those were the darkest days of my life. After doing everything I thought I could do to hide my addiction, even relocating to different cities, I discovered two things. The first thing I discovered is that I could not hide from myself. Everywhere I went, there I was. Even moving from city to city, State to State, it seemed like I met me there. Along with meeting me I immediately met people just like me, addicts and alcoholics. I was like a human magnet, attracting all the wrong people who were doing all the wrong things, however, the things that addiction drove me to do.

The second thing I learned was that I could not hide from God. How silly of me to think that the Man who created me could not see and even feel everything I was doing. While using drugs and alcohol, shame and guilt set in and I could feel the disappointment God must have had in me. I would ask myself, how God could love a sinner like me.

Unbeknownst to me I being was given the ultimate proof that He loved me. After losing all and I mean all, family, self respect, self esteem, my mind, car, jobs, and my home I found myself in a state of despair and deep depression. After several overdoses, He rescued me and set me free and I have not use any drugs or drank alcohol since that one faithful night.

Am I perfect?, oh no not by a long shot, but my love for God and His love for me prevents me from living in darkness and I can see His Marvelous Light. TGIF!!

Luke 5:20 New American Standard Bible (NASB)
[20] Seeing their faith, He said, "Friend, your sins are forgiven you."

PERSONAL REFLECTION:

_____

_____

_____

_____

_____

_____

_____

_____

_____

_____

_____

_____

_____

_____

For it is by grace you have been saved,
through faith ; and this not from
yourselves, it is the gift of God;
not by works, so that no one can boast.
(Ephesians 2:8 , 9)

Reflection 3

<u>Ephesians 2:8-9</u> For by grace you have been saved through faith; and that not of yourselves, *it is* the gift of God; [9] not as a result of works, so that no one may boast.

Reflecting is awesome; this scripture is the first scripture with more than two or three words that I was able to memorize. How proud I was especially when I really understood what I had memorized. For so many years I thought I had the power. I thought that it was me running the show. I just knew that when things did go right in my life I should take the credit for it. How very wrong I was. I had no idea that it was the Grace of God that sustained and maintained me. How could I have ever believed that it was me that rescued me from kidnapping, relieved me of depression, allowed me to survive more than one suicide attempt, allowed my children to survive and thrive in spite of me. How grandiose I was to even think that it was me who delivered me from alcohol and drug addiction and all of the behaviors that accompanied it. Let the truth be known, I only acknowledged that there was a God when I needed someone to blame for the jackpots that I got myself into. Therefore, it wasn't even my own faith that saw me through; it was the prayers of grandma and so many others. It was their faith and the sounds of their prayers that God heard. Humbly, I thank you Lord for the Gift of Your Son, Jesus Christ.

Amazing Grace, how sweet the sound,
That saved a wretch like me.
I once was lost but now am found,
Was blind, but now I see.

T'was Grace that taught my heart to fear.
And Grace, my fears relieved.
How precious did that Grace appear
The hour I first believed…

John Newton (1725-1807)

PERSONAL REFLECTION:

What, then, shall we say in response to these things?

If God is for us, who can be against us?

Romans 8:31

Reflection 4

Romans 8:31- What then shall we say to these things? If God *is* for us, who *is* against us?

The times have been numerous, times where I have been judged, convicted and crucified by the words and thoughts of others. There have been times when even my best intentions were seen as wrong leading to being talked about, criticized, and shunned by those I love dearly.

In life, I have found myself lost deep in self pity with feelings that sometimes have been indescribable. As much as I hate to admit it, I felt so low that I wanted to end it all. I thought that if I were no longer around others would be happy. That old adage "out of sight, out of mind" was what I believed was the solution. I was so lost in my own way of thinking I thought I could never be found.

I can't tell you exactly when it happened but a sense of heightened esteem and self love manifested. I repeated affirmation after affirmation, I prayed and I prayed, I cried and I cried. The scales disappeared from my eyes. Gratefully, one day the self pity disappeared. The pain was gone and a smile appeared on my face and in my heart. I realized that my joy did not nor could ever come from man/woman. Joy comes only from my relationship with God. I have an awesome relationship with my Daddy, He loves me and I love Him. "Joy, the world didn't give it and world can't take it away" (This Joy I Have by Shirley Caesar).

PERSONAL REFLECTION:

_____

_____

_____

_____

_____

_____

_____

_____

_____

_____

_____

_____

_____

_____

"FOR I **know the plans** I HAVE FOR YOU," DECLARES THE LORD, "PLANS TO **prosper you** AND NOT TO HARM YOU, PLANS TO GIVE YOU **hope** AND A **future.**"

JEREMIAH 29:11

Reflection 5

Jeremiah 29:11-12 For I know the plans that I have for you,' declares the LORD, 'plans for welfare and not for calamity to give you a future and a hope. [12] Then you will call upon Me and come and pray to Me, and I will listen to you.

That one faithful night, it was November 1, 1989, you heard me, thank you Father, you heard me. I cried out to you and you answered my prayers. It was a simple prayer "God, help me" but you knew it was a sincere prayer and you came and rescued me.

Not too many things had gone right for me for since 1966 to that date. It was in 1966 that I made a declaration to God that I was going to run my own life. My plan was to do what I wanted, when I wanted, how I wanted and with whom I wanted.

 You see, I had lost my best friend, my Aunt who helped raised me had died. Deep down inside I felt that she was really the only one who loved me because she was there for me morning, night, in sickness, during fears she wiped my tears, she taught me so much. She sent me to Church even though she never accompanied me. She healed my wombs and held my hand when I felt lost and alone. She was my everything. At the age of 12 I had no concept of death, its rhyme or reason totally eluded me.

It was during this time of grief as I know it now I turned into a stranger even to myself. I began hanging out with the wild crowd at school. My straight A grades dropped. I knew something was wrong but was not willing to make any changes. This path of destruction went on for the next 23 years, 23 years of turmoil, drama, destruction, and devastation. How ironic, as I type these very words, November 1, 2014 I am less than an hour from my 25th year of deliverance from alcohol and other drugs.

You see, God interceded on the plans I had for myself. He allowed me to think I was running my own life long enough for me to finally come to the realization that it was not true at all. Actually, He had been interceding all the time; I know this now because if it had not been for His Grace and Mercy, I would have been dead long ago.

Today I live a good life, not a perfect life, because I am not a perfect person. But the life I live is far better than anything that I could have planned for myself.

Who would have thought... From Addict to Author.

PERSONAL REFLECTION:

_____

_____

_____

_____

_____

_____

_____

_____

_____

_____

_____

_____

Philippians 4:6-7

Do not be anxious about anything,
but in every situation,
through prayer and petition,
with thanksgiving,
present your requests to God.
And the peace of God,
which transcends all understanding,
will guard your hearts and minds
in Christ Jesus.

Reflection 6

Philippians 4:6-7 Don't worry about anything; instead, pray about everything. Tell God what you need, and thank him for all he has done. Then you will experience God's peace, which exceeds anything we can understand. His peace will guard your hearts and minds as you live in Christ Jesus.

Only God knows all of my worries and my fears and I am so grateful that He does not stop loving me even during the times where my faith falters. Not only does He love me, He rescues me. What a blessing from my Heavenly Father.

Patience is not always a Fruit of the Spirit that I demonstrate, I look for instant gratification. I want what I want and I want it now.

Not using being "human" as an excuse, there are no excuses, but it happens, there are times when I didn't think I would make it through. There have been times when I gave up. There have been times when desperation set in to the point that I thought that taking my own life was the only answer. Yes, not only have suicidal ideations set in, but attempts have also occurred, more than once.

The miracle, the blessing connected to this reflection is this; even when I couldn't pray for myself, even when I couldn't tell God exactly what I needed, or know how to thank Him for what He was going to do, the Holy Spirit was interceding on my behalf.

Today, I worry less, I pray more, I read my Bible more and I trust more. I have learned to thank Him in advance for what only He knows He has planned for me. God is leading me in some miraculous directions, places that I could never have imaged with my finite mind. I talk to God on a regular basis about where He is taking me and His answer is this; don't worry about where you are going...just trust me and believe that it is all for your good.

PERSONAL REFLECTION:

_____

_____

_____

_____

_____

_____

_____

_____

_____

_____

_____

_____

The Prayer Of Jabez

And Jabez called on the God Of Israel, saying,

Oh that thou would bless me indeed, and enlarge my

coast, and that thine hand might be with me, and that

thou wouldest keep me from evil, that it may not grieve me!

And God granted him that which he requested.

1 Chronicles 4:10

Reflection 7

1 CHRONICLES 4:10 Now Jabez called on the God of Israel, saying, "Oh that You would bless me indeed and enlarge my border, and that Your hand might be with me, and that You would keep *me* from harm that *it* may not pain me!" And God granted him what he requested.

...and God granted what I requested. I can't even count how many times He has granted my requests. Just so very many. Every time I think of the goodness of the Lord my soul just shouts out with joy. Even though I must admit that during my years of active addiction the only times I acknowledged God was after I got myself into trouble. Either I was blaming Him for what had happened or I was begging for Him to get me out of it.

Today, I know that my begging was actually praying, petitioning Him for help. And each and every time He granted my requests. The answers to my prayers did not always come as quickly as I wanted but they surely did come. At 23 years of active addiction to alcohol, marijuana, heroin, pills, cocaine and last but surely not least crack cocaine I was in the perfect position for deliverance. I sat alone in the dark crying and all I could say was "Help Me". I was bankrupt in every area of my life, mentally, emotionally, spiritually, financially, and physically, I had only two options; Deliverance or Death. Again, I called out "Help Me". And He did just that, not the way I thought the help would come but His hand was upon me and it came.

25 years later, I am free, free from me. My help comes from the Lord and that I have no doubt. I am blessed indeed to be alive and thriving in every aspect of my life, even those that don't look like they are thriving. I know that God is working it all out and it will be worked out in His time, not mine. OH, HOW HE LOVES ME!!

PERSONAL REFLECTION:

_____

_____

_____

_____

_____

_____

_____

_____

_____

_____

_____

_____

_____

I CAN DO ALL THINGS THROUGH CHRIST WHO STRENGTHENS ME.

PHILIPPIANS 4:13

Reflection 8

PHILIPPIANS 4:13 I can do all things through Him who strengthens me.

Not only is this scripture a demonstration of God's love, it is also an awesome promise to those who love and believe in Him.

This promise came and continues to come true for me even when I did not realize that it was not me that had any strength of my own. It was years and years of getting it all wrong, experiencing self inflicted pain and suffering, delusionally thinking that I had it all together before I realized that I could not do this thing called life all alone, I needed Him, I needed His strength.

I was told not once but many times that I was insane, defining insanity as doing the same things over and over again and expecting different (better) results.

As I reflect upon toxic relationships that I experienced, I can surely see now just how insane I was. I realize that I was looking for love in all the wrong places and doing all the wrong things to get it. I was entirely clueless. I didn't know that I didn't have to accept sex when I wanted love. I had no idea of what my true worth was or could have been. I faked the funk, talked the talk, and wore the masks to hide my feelings of inferiority, loneliness and powerlessness. Have you ever been at a party loaded with people laughing, talking, dancing and sometimes doing other things and it seemed as if you were the only person in the room? If you nodded your head or said yes, you know how I felt.

But then there was the time for a come up. How does that work, who is going to help me, where am I going and what am I going to do when I get there?

I finally wanted to do better but again I was clueless!! But He Loves Me…. Even though where He took me was not where I wanted to be, I had to remember that it was me who was asking for help…He didn't need my help that's for sure.

Today, everything I do, every breath I breathe, every step I make, the she who I am now, confident and full of power is because He loves me enough to give me strength.

PERSONAL REFLECTION:

A THOUSAND MAY FALL AT YOUR SIDE, TEN THOUSAND AT YOUR RIGHT HAND, BUT IT WILL NOT COME NEAR YOU.

Reflection 9

PSALM 91:7 A thousand may fall at your side And ten thousand at your right hand, *But* it shall not approach you.

His Love protected me, my soul cries out...Thank you, thank you, thank you. Have you ever realized that something you thought was a nuisance or from the devil really happened for your own good? Well, I find myself giving the enemy too much credit in too many circumstances.

What started out as a normal work day, something happened. I received a message of love from God so loud and clear that it actually startled me. But more than the shock was the peace that came with the message.

I returned to my car from seeing a client, I opened the door, sat in the seat, put my seat belt on, put the key in the ignition and there was silence, dead silence. No humming of the engine, no click, click, click, nothing!!

My natural emotion would have been anger in this type of situation. I would probably scream and swear and blame the enemy for infringing on my all too busy schedule. How dare my car not start when I have so many appointments to keep, people to see and things to do, not to mention the money I would lose by having to sit still.

But something supernatural happened this morning. I turned the key in the ignition a couple of more times, still nothing.
Then came that supernatural message that brought peace way beyond my understanding. The message was "God blocked it!" God had blocked a situation unknown to me

that I would have encountered had my car started and I had gone on with my schedule.

My question to me was, how many times had He "blocked it? How many times had I wanted to turn right but turned left instead because He was protecting me?

PERSONAL REFLECTION:

_____

_____

_____

_____

_____

_____

_____

_____

_____

_____

_____

_____

_____

"Ye are of **God**, little children, and have overcome them: because **great**er **is** he that **is** in you, than he that **is** in the world"

Reflection 10

1 JOHN 4:4 You are of God, little children, and have overcome them, because He who is in you is greater than he who is in the world.

Oh how He loves me, oh my, what a declaration of love, only God would tell me how great I am and really mean it. Yes, of course some family and friends will pat you on the back, but when God tells me how great I am I know for sure, without any doubt that it is true.

I don't have to do anything to prove my greatness. He tells me that I am great at my highest and my lowest. I am great because I am of God. It is Him in me that makes me great.

We have all encountered people in our lives who give us accolades, attaboys, compliments and such. However, in some cases, I'm not going to say most, but some, there are motives and hidden agendas behind those pats on the back.

I reflect with laughter upon the days when I was using drugs and alcohol. I got plenty of pats on the back, especially on pay day when I would set up the bar or buy the dope. It was funny how I attracted all the wrong people who would say all the right things.

Overcoming the world is a great accomplishment although not so easy. I had become so used to and sometimes even proud of what the world thought and said about me that I lost the real me, the me that God says I am.

Today, I am who I am, I am who He says I am.. I AM GREAT!!

PERSONAL REFLECTION:

_____

_____

_____

_____

_____

_____

_____

_____

_____

_____

_____

FOR YOU CREATED MY INMOST BEING

YOU KNIT ME TOGETHER IN MY

MOTHER'S WOMB

I PRAISE YOU BECAUSE I AM

fearfully and wonderfully made

YOUR WORKS ARE

wonderful

I KNOW THAT FULL WELL

PSALM 139:13-14

Reflection 11

Psalm 139:13-14 For You formed my inward parts; You wove me in my mother's womb. I will give thanks to You, for I am fearfully and wonderfully made; Wonderful are Your works, And my soul knows it very well.

Yes, that's me, fearfully and wonderfully made. In spite of how I have seen myself in the past, no matter what I have done to myself, no matter how far down the scale I have gone... I am special. He created me, He didn't have to do it, but He did.

If this scripture isn't an esteem builder, nothing is. When I am feeling at my lowest I can read and reflect on this passage to build me up like never before.

Low or no self esteem was evidenced in my life for years. And to be totally transparent, it can still plague me today if I'm not careful.

Those feelings of self loathing were very apparent in my life of addiction. Who in the world would do the things I did to myself and say "I Love Me". Talk about delusional, OMGoodness, to the fullest. All of the things I did to my mind, body, and spirit and soul were ridiculous.

However, having had a spiritual experience and being able to see through spiritual lenses I began to live the life that God wants me to live. I have began to see the reason for who I am, what I was, why I went through what I went through and my present purpose. It is so important for me to know and understand where I have been, therefore, know where I am and where I am going.

PERSONAL REFLECTION:

_____

_____

_____

_____

_____

_____

_____

_____

_____

_____

_____

I have LOVED you
with an everlasting
LOVE
Therefore with
LOVINGKINDNESS
I have drawn you.

JEREMIAH 31:3

Reflection 12

Jeremiah 31:3 The LORD appeared to him from afar, *saying*, "I have loved you with an everlasting love; Therefore I have drawn you with lovingkindness

Unconditional love, it's amazing that no matter how much I have done to harm myself and others; God still loves me with an everlasting love. A love that never fails and will never end.

What have I done to deserve, everlasting love? Nothing of my own doing or without paying a price. I know of few people who have loved me without conditions, there are some, and they know who they are. However, even they have not always understood me, especially during my personal times of mayhem, gloom and self defeating behaviors.

Unmerited, unwarranted, undeserved, yet everlasting love is what my God has given me all the days of my life.

I reflect upon the days that I even gave up on myself, days where I had no clue as to who I was or why I was. I felt totally unnecessary. Of course I didn't know whose I was because I so full of self pity and self loathing.

Self pity to the point of not wanting to go on. Suicide, yes, that's the answer. You might call it the easy way out, I saw it as the only way out. Several times I tried to end it all. Over the years when one method didn't work, I would try another, carbon monoxide poisoning (asphyxiation), attempt to be hit by a bus, and pill overdose.

I am so grateful for the fact that Jesus died so that I could live. Believe me every day is not the best day for me. However, every day I look for something greater to happen and yes, every day that I live and breathe, I am so happy that God's everlasting love prevented my attempts to die to manifest.

PERSONAL REFLECTION:

_____

_____

_____

_____

_____

_____

_____

_____

_____

_____

_____

_____

Who is he that condemns?
It is Christ that died,
yes rather, that is risen again,
who is even at
the right hand of God,
who also makes
intercession
for us.

~ Romans 8:34

Reflection 13

Romans 8:34- Who will condemn them? Christ has died, and more importantly, he was brought back to life. Christ is in the honored position—the one next to God the Father on the heavenly throne. Christ also intercedes for us.

It was a beautiful summer day or at least it would seem that way to the average person. The sun was shining, people were happy, laughing and having fun. What seemed like an average day at work where my co-workers were serving their clients and going about their ordinary routines, deep down inside I was miserable. I talked with a co-worker about some of the things I was feeling but my words seemed to fall upon deaf ears. Nevertheless, I was able to talk to someone. However, despite the talk, I still felt lonely, alone and empty inside.

I was going through some emotional turmoil, signs and symptoms were evident. I made many attempts to fake it through but it wasn't working. What I thought was a breakthrough at one time was actually the beginning of a breakdown.

I found that people, co-workers, including people I thought were friends saw the signs, but found it funny.

Depression defined by Wikipedia: Major depressive disorder (MDD) (also known as clinical depression, major depression, unipolar depression, or unipolar disorder; or as recurrent depression in the case of repeated episodes) is a mental disorder characterized by a pervasive and persistent low mood that is accompanied by low self-esteem and by a loss of interest or pleasure in normally enjoyable activities. The term "depression" is used in a number of different ways. It is often used to mean this syndrome but may refer to other mood disorders or simply to a low mood. Major depressive disorder is a disabling condition that adversely affects a person's family, work or school life, sleeping and eating habits, and general health. In the United States, around 3.4% of people with major depression commit suicide, and up to 60% of people who commit suicide had depression or another mood disorder.

PERSONAL REFLECTION:

_____

_____

_____

_____

_____

_____

_____

_____

_____

_____

_____

_____

_____

"he saved us, not because of works done by us in righteousness, but according to his own mercy, by the washing of regeneration and renewal of the Holy Spirit."
Titus 3:5

Reflection 14

Titus 3:4 But after that the kindness and love of God our Saviour toward man appeared,

If you have ever experienced depression you know the feelings I was experiencing. If haven't gone through depression, you cannot even imagine the inner turmoil a person goes through.

Initially, despite being a therapist, I didn't recognize the symptoms in myself. Yes, I knew things in my life were not going as I wished, I wasn't happy, but Major Depression never entered my mind.

After work, that beautiful summer day, I went home and just sat and cried. I had been used to getting on the internet (pre-Facebook) and chatting with friends whom I thought could not see or feel me. Yes, we had some meaningful conversations usually of the religious type. But there were times when they made me laugh. I had and still do have a special group that are from the UK, I felt safe chatting with them because as I said I never thought I would meet them face to face. I could hide behind my computer monitor and no one would ever know.

Or so I thought.

It was the next morning and I set out with a plan in mind. My plan went something like this. I had two bottles of pills, pretty strong pain pills and antidepressants. I called off of work reporting that I was not feeling well. I put the pills and a glass of water on the side of my computer table. Next, what I thought would be my last check of my emails.

I then, habitually, went into the chat room where I and my UK friends would hang out.

My plan was to have my last conversation with them or with anyone else.

PERSONAL REFLECTION:

_____

_____

_____

_____

_____

_____

_____

_____

_____

_____

_____

_____

GOD WILL WRECK YOUR PLANS WHEN HE SEES THAT YOUR PLANS ARE ABOUT TO WRECK YOU

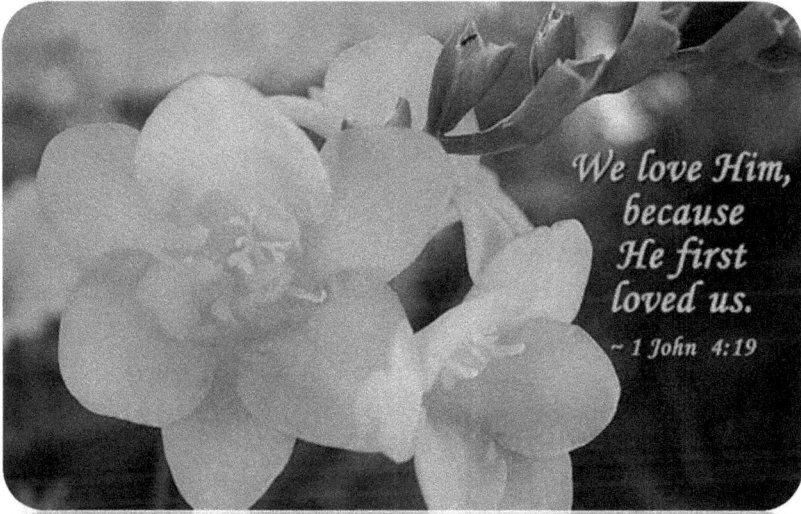

We love Him, because He first loved us.
~ 1 John 4:19

Reflection 15

1 John 4:9 In this was manifested the love of God toward us, because that God sent his only begotten Son into the world, that we might live through him.

Yesterday I told you about my plans. Yes, my plans. Well, as the picture says and believe me it is so true, God will wreck your plans when He sees that your plans are about to wreck you and let me tell you, he wrecked my plans in such a smooth manner that I was in complete awe of His mercy and grace.

Well, that conversation that I thought would be my last turned out to be the end of yet another new beginning and it went something like this: The instant messenger chimed...

Ray: Good morning Tina, how are you doing this morning?
Me: Ray, I am doing alright. (I was not about to tell him my plans)
Ray: Are you sure?
Me: Yes Ray, I am just fine. (As I look at the bottles of pills)
Ray: God told me that I need to pray for you this morning, would you like to join me?
Me: No, but actually you can go right ahead. I need to get to work soon. (I was lying through my teeth)
Ray: Ok and he proceeded to pray the most sincere prayer that I had heard him pray in a long time.
Me: After about 10 minutes of prayer... I interrupted and said Amen, thinking that saying Amen would end the praying. I then said, Ray I have something to do right now, I have to go.

Ray: Ok, just a sec. (The man prayed for at least another 15 minutes)
Me: I'm praying to myself, oh God, would you please shut his mouth, now!! Thank you Ray, I really have to go now.
Ray: Continued to pray...

Well, let me tell you that by the time Ray finished praying, the compulsion to take my life was gone, it had totally disappeared. In fact I was so drained (in a good way) from Ray's prayers, that all I wanted to do was to go to sleep naturally.

Yeah, God wrecked my plans that morning. It was years before I told Ray how God had used him to save my life. We then prayed together as we had done so many times before.

PERSONAL REFLECTION:

_____

_____

_____

_____

_____

_____

_____

_____

_____

_____

_____

_____

_____

Reflection 16

Matthew 10:30-31 But the very hairs of your head are all numbered.
Fear ye not therefore, ye are of more value than many sparrows.

There is nothing nor anybody that could ever convince me that there is not power in prayer. When God has placed someone in your life that is so in tuned to your inner most being don't ever take them for granted. Since that faithful morning the friendship between Ray and I have lasted over the years and in spite of the thousands of miles between us.

Part of Ray's prayer was his praying about how precious I was in God's sight. He prayed about what a privilege it was to be a child of the Living God. He prayed about the awesome things that God had in store for me. He prayed my continued salvation and manifestation of my love for God.

You see, I had not stopped loving God, I had just stopped loving me which was a result of the depression that had manifested in me. Depression took me somewhere that I really didn't want to be and almost took me somewhere that I could not return from.

As time passed I was able to see how precious I actually was in God's sight. God chose to create me, He knew me before I knew myself. He formed me in my mother's womb. I was not a mistake. No, I was not a mistake, I was not a bastard. I am my Daddy's little girl and I am fearfully and wonderfully made.

He took the time to make me who I am from the top of my head to the tip of my toes.

Yes, I am more valuable that the sparrows and today I chose to show my gratitude by being the best that my God has meant for me to be.

PERSONAL REFLECTION:

_____

_____

_____

_____

_____

_____

_____

_____

_____

_____

_____

The bravest thing I ever did was continuing my life when I wanted to die.

No, despite all these things,

overwhelming

VICTORY

is ours *through Christ*,

who *loved* us.

Romans 8:37

Reflection 17

Romans 8:37-39 - No, in all these things we are more than conquerors through him who loved us. For I am sure that neither death nor life, nor angels nor rulers, nor things present nor things to come, nor powers, nor height nor depth, nor anything else in all creation, will be able to separate us from the love of God in Christ Jesus our Lord.

This page is surely one that I must not only reflect upon but pray on relentlessly. Lord knows I do my human best to honor my God by fighting the battlefield that continuingly wages war in my head.

Believe me days of depression occasionally set in, however, the difference from that day that Ray prayed me back to life and today is that I don't keep those feelings bottled up inside of me.

Today, I reach out; I call, text, inbox, and tell others what I am feeling. I never want to feel that way I felt that morning with the pills sitting next to me.

Spiritual help is also available; it's just a knee bend away. If it's professional help you need obtain it, just keep in mind that there is nothing that you have to go through alone.

No matter what the situation, circumstance, thought, feeling, emotion, behavior, or anything else that may try to distract me, I must always remember that He loves me. I must remember that I am strong through Him who is the giver of all things. There can be nothing to change my belief, that all things are possible through Him that gives me strength.

PERSONAL REFLECTION:

_____

_____

_____

_____

_____

_____

_____

_____

_____

_____

_____

But because of his
great love for us,
God, who is rich
in mercy,
made us alive
with Christ
even when we were
dead in transgressions~
it is by grace
you have been saved.
Ephesians 2:4-5

Reflection 18

Ephesians 2:4-5 But God, being rich in mercy, because of the great love with which he loved us, even when we were dead in our trespasses, made us alive together with Christ— by grace you have been saved

Oh I sit here tonight and I sing and I sing and I sing. How blessed I am that God saw fit to love me in spite of me.

What a blessing it is to know that no matter who I am, what I've done or what I've gone through, by Grace I have been saved.

I accepted Christ at an early age, even though as you have read, there were times you couldn't see it or would you believe it.

I had a thirst and a hunger to be who God wanted me to be. I gave up all my worldly possessions, I changed the way I treated people, and I stopped looking up to those negative, thrilling people who I thought I wanted to be like.

But I let self get in the way and it took me on a very long detour of self will run riot. It took a long time for me to get back on the right path. Now don't get it twisted I didn't become a saint, but I can say, I'm not who I want to be but thank God I'm not who I used to be. In fact, I think I am right where I am supposed to be right now.

Tonight I just want to say THANK YOU LORD; I don't look like what I've been through. I am no longer the walking dead. I am alive and glad about it--- tonight I sing and I rejoice!!

PERSONAL REFLECTION:

_____

_____

_____

_____

_____

_____

_____

_____

_____

_____

_____

_____

YEA, THOUGH I WALK THROUGH THE
VALLEY OF THE SHADOW OF DEATH,
I WILL FEAR NO EVIL;

FOR YOU ARE WITH ME;
YOUR ROD & YOUR STAFF,
THEY COMFORT ME.

PSALM 23:4

Reflection 19

Psalm 23:4 Even though I walk through the valley of the shadow of death,
I fear no evil, for You are with me; Your rod and Your staff, they comfort me.

Walking through the valley was not the hard part. You see, I was used to the valley experiences. I was used to the negative people, places and things. In fact the more negative the situation the more thrilled I was.

Going into unknown drug situations, the after hour establishments, the fights, the shootings, everything associated with the "life" was where I thought I was supposed to be.

Allowing God to turn my life around was the hard part. I had become accustomed to a certain lifestyle for such a long time and that is what became normal to me. Yes, being abnormal was normal.

The journey from being hopeless to sharing hope with others was a road surely less traveled by me.

I wanted so badly to fit in somewhere that I lost myself in the process. I feared very few things and I surely wasn't afraid of the devil, I actually believed that he was my friend. Well why wouldn't I when I didn't believe that God loved me.

What an idiot I was, I was clueless that I was the walking dead and it was God alone, all by himself that saved me, in spite of me. Because He Loves Me.

PERSONAL REFLECTION:

_____

_____

_____

_____

_____

_____

_____

_____

_____

_____

_____

_____

Cast all your worries ON HIM, BECAUSE He cares FOR YOU.

1 Peter 5:7

Reflection 20

1 Peter 5:6-7 Humble yourselves, therefore, under the mighty hand of God so that at the proper time he may exalt you, casting all your anxieties on him, because he cares for you.

I have had my days. Days that I just couldn't see the sun shine. There were days where I didn't think there was a way out, to pay those bills, to buy groceries, to put gas in the tank, or put an extra five dollars in the collection bucket at Church.

What about those days when I didn't feel loved by the ones I loved the most?

Well let me tell you about The Comforter, The Man who not only delivers but makes a way out of no way. The Comforter who does not work in mysterious ways, He just works and works it out perfectly. Let me tell you about The Man who delivers a check to my mailbox just when I need it. Let me tell you about The Man who sends a friend to bring me a plate of food when I'm hungry. Don't get me started telling you about the goodness of my Lord. Let me tell you about The Man who lets me find money on the ground to put gas in the tank, when the needle is below "E". What about that Sunday morning when I put on a skirt or pair of pants I haven't worn in a while and find money in the pockets?

Jehovah Jireh, my Provider, The Man who not only brought me out but lifted me up and above all that I could ever imagine. I am blessed beyond measure and I know full well that my blessings didn't come to me because I was such a good person or because of the good deeds I had performed.

The blessings of the Lord are mine because it's my time. I was born for such a time as this. I was born for right now to be all that He has purposed me to be.

Yes, again I declare that He has brought me from "addict to author" because He loves me.

PERSONAL REFLECTION:

_____

_____

_____

_____

_____

_____

_____

_____

_____

_____

_____

For I am
the perfect Father.

Matthew 5:48

Reflection 21

Matthew 5:48 But you are to be perfect, even as your Father in heaven is perfect.

What comes to mind is this; when the same thoughts come to mind and you're stuck in a situation that you thought you had gotten over, the thoughts may be the same, but God's answer will always be the same. "I will never, leave you or forsake you". I had no idea of how deep my desire to have a earthly father really was. But I do remember, receiving the same response through two different people that God put in my life.

Tonight as I write, I reflect only upon the thought of my being in my mother's womb. You all may have heard the old saying "I came into the world alone and so shall I leave this world alone".

But what about the time in between the dash? Was I meant to be alone? Of course not. I was not born to be or feel alone or lonely. However, those times did occur.

Some of the loneliest times in my life were when I watched my friends with their fathers. They looked so happy and complete. Being raised in Chicago, seeing two parent homes was not the norm for me. So when I would see my friends living in homes with both parents I experienced several different emotions the most prominent ones being ones of sadness and loneliness.

Now don't get me wrong or feel sorry for me, I was raised in a very loving home even though I have to admit I didn't always appreciate it. I was the type of little girl that always wanted more. You can call me spoiled because in most cases I got what I wanted.

I felt that I was supposed to have more. Today, that's a good thing because when I want more I know how to work for it. But that was not the case when I was a child.

I wanted to have a father, I wanted what my friends had, I wanted what my friends had and not having it made me sad. I would be asked about my father and I couldn't say anything because I didn't know who or where he was.

I asked and asked and never got an answer. Even as an adult I often wondered about the other side of me. Did I act like him, did I look like him? I don't know. What I do know is that for years I looked for the love of a father in all the wrong places.

But what I found out while in drug and alcohol treatment was that it really didn't matter who my biological father was. I was told that I surely didn't have to get high or have sex with men I didn't even like as a substitute for the love of human father.

My counselor looked me in the face and told me that she could feel the pain that I was experiencing as I talked about my feelings for the first time in my life. What she preceded to tell me changed my life. I looked at her peculiarly as she told me that I had always had a father.

She told me that God was my Father and that He loved me in a way that no earthly father could ever love me. She told me that He had always been there and that I should never feel alone. I will be forever grateful to this lady who didn't proclaim to be religious but believed that she would not have survived her own battle with addiction without God. I listened intently as I was taught the true meaning of the word "father". Not the dictionary definition but the Biblical definition.

I don't have to feel alone or lonely, I have no need to be sad, I don't have to be jealous, I don't need to wonder who my earthly father is.

From the womb (from which He formed me) to the tomb (to which I will return to Him) I will be forever grateful to my heavenly Father from whom all blessings flow.

My Heavenly Daddy is The Perfect Father and yes, I am Daddy's little girl.

PERSONAL REFLECTION:

I HAVE BEEN
CRUCIFIED WITH CHRIST;
IT IS NO LONGER I WHO LIVE,
BUT CHRIST LIVES IN ME;

AND THE LIFE WHICH I
NOW LIVE IN THE FLESH
I LIVE BY FAITH
IN THE SON OF GOD,
**WHO LOVED ME
& GAVE HIMSELF
FOR ME.**

GALATIANS 2:20

Reflection 22

Galatians 2:20 I have been crucified with Christ. It is no longer I who live, but Christ who lives in me and the life I now live in the flesh I live by faith in the Son of God. Who loved me and gave himself for me.

With Vision comes an Assignment, and Lord knows He gave me one heck of an assignment. When sitting on the side of that cot and I said that one simple prayer Help Me", He answered me, not really how I was expecting it, but nonetheless, an answer.

A chain of events were set into place. I have been on a Mission to help others. And that is why I am here right now writing, I was sent to tell you that no matter how far down you have gone, you can GET UP!!. You were born for such a time as this, a time where you and only you can make an impact on the lives of hundreds, thousands, even millions who don't think they have what it takes to live a peaceful life.

Live God's Purpose, Realize Your Vision and Create your own Goal or Mission and GO for it, THE SKY IS THE FOR WHAT YOU CAN HAVE!!

The things used to do I don't do any more. Who would have thought 25 years ago that I would become a social worker, author, talk show host, event planner, mentor, and an encourager with a deep love for others? How did all of this happen? It happened because God loves me.

PERSONAL REFLECTION:

_____

_____

_____

_____

_____

_____

_____

_____

_____

_____

_____

_____

_____

_____

Dry Bones
one revealed
kingdom tomb indeed God's shepherd
give David death raised bodies dead Spirit
Christ Pharisees J covenant everlasting Hebrew die dry new visions beautiful place
Jesus buried within
Resurrection together alive Ezekiel's context writing make name people put men servant king
Israel dwells heart enjoy
life body live Ezekiel faith LORD resurrection
Christ's Apostles prophesied flesh returned resurrected Church
eternal saved

Valley bones

Reflection 23

Ezekiel 37:1-14 [Vision *of the Valley of Dry Bones*] The hand of the LORD was upon me, and He brought me out by the Spirit of the LORD and set me down in the middle of the valley; and it was full of bones. He caused me to pass among them round about, and behold, *there were* very many on the surface of the valley; and lo, *they were* very dry. He said to me, "Son of man, can these bones live?" And I answered, "O Lord GOD, You know.".....

For Ezekiel, it was a vision but for me it is a reality. Can these bones live? Yes they can. I am a living testimony of dry bones being brought back to life.

I know today that all things are possible with God and He has proved that in my life time and time again. He has not only saved my life but He has brought me back to life. He has given me the precious gift of being able to breathe again. I am not just talking about a figurative breath but a literal breath. I have to keep mentioning the attempts to take my life because today I am so very grateful to be alive and I never want to forget. I am grateful that God would not let me die. His hand has been upon me from the very beginning and He has never let me go.

Even when I was at my worse, He cradled me in His loving arms.

I have been to funerals of those that I used drugs with even worse I still see others that are still using. I look at them and wonder why God saved me from that devastation and not them. Well those who have passed on have been saved but what about the living dead? What are His plans for them? I don't know and I guess I am not supposed to know. What I do know is that I am meant to be an example of God's love for me and for them.

PERSONAL REFLECTION:

_____

_____

_____

_____

_____

_____

_____

_____

_____

_____

_____

GOD HAS FORGIVEN ALL YOUR MISTAKES.

PSALM 103:12

Reflection 24

<u>Psalm 103:10-14</u> He does not deal with us according to our sins, nor repay us according to our iniquities. For as high as the heavens are above the earth, so great is his steadfast love toward those who fear him; as far as the east is from the west, so far does he remove our transgressions from us. As a father shows compassion to his children, so the Lord shows compassion to those who fear him. For he knows our frame; he remembers that we are dust.

I am in awe of Martin Luther King, Jr.'s quote and much as I am in David's account of forgiveness.

Martin Luther King, Jr.said "We must develop and maintain the capacity to forgive. He who is devoid of the power to forgive is devoid of the power to love. There is some good in the worst of us and some evil in the best of us. When we discover this, we are less prone to hate our enemies".

Tearfully, I reflect upon the great struggle I have had with not so much forgiving others, but with forgiving myself. What David and Dr. King are saying to me is without forgiveness there is no love.

I am blessed to have come to the conclusion that it has been easier to forgive others because no one has ever hurt me as much as I have hurt myself. I have always been my own worst enemy. I would not even dare let anyone harm me the way I have harmed myself.

God has already forgiven me so who am I not to forgive myself. "For as far as the heavens are above the earth", how profound and how beautiful.

Yes I am Beautiful, Yes I am Worthy of Forgiveness, Yes I am Forgiven, not because of anything special I have done but because He Loves Me just the way I am flaws and all.

I have to practice forgiveness diligently as my mind often takes me back to my past, to that dark place that held no good thing.

I have to use positive affirmations daily to remind myself that I am Daddy's little girl and I am not who I used to be, I am a new creation in Christ Jesus.

Here are a few of the affirmations that I recite:

I am enough
I am love
I will not accept sex when I want love/marriage
I love who I see in the mirror
This is just the beginning
I will achieve my goals
Something Greater is Happening in My Life Today
God loves me and I will love myself

PERSONAL REFLECTION:

_____

_____

_____

_____

_____

_____

_____

_____

_____

_____

_____

_____

_____

_____

Colossians 2:6-7 (KJV)

As ye have therefore received Christ Jesus the Lord, so walk ye in him:7 Rooted and built up in him, and stablished in the faith, as ye have been taught, abounding therein with thanksgiving.

Reflection 25

Colossians 2:6-7 *Therefore* as you have received Christ Jesus the Lord, so walk in Him, having been firmly rooted and now being built up in Him and established in your faith, just as you were instructed, and overflowing with gratitude.

Always wanting more than I had, always wanting to be somewhere where I wasn't, always looking outside of myself for people, places and things to make me happy. I married very young and had my first child at the age of 16. I was a frightened little girl who dared to tell anyone that I didn't know how to be a wife or mother. I tried to fake it but I just couldn't. I made a decision (not a good one) to leave my family. I literally abandoned my family for a bottle of wine and a motorcycle club. Feelings of loss and confusion led to even more desperation on my part. I turned to sex, alcohol and drugs at an early age to fill the empty void. I didn't think God would or could ever smile on me. How could He?

I would come down from a binge and shame and guilt was there. They were ever present reminding me of my pitiful life. How many many times I could not look in a mirror because of not wanting to see what I had become. I would continually ask myself the question "why can't I change, why can't I give love the way I wanted to"?

The answer to that question was plain; I had not learned to love myself, so how could I really love anyone else? I was always looking for someone to do for me what I couldn't do for myself.

I smile now as I can say that I know God and it is in knowing Him that I can accept His unconditional love for me and thus love others.

PERSONAL REFLECTION:

Praise be to the God
and Father of our
Lord Jesus Christ!

In his great mercy
he has given us new birth
into a living hope
through the resurrection of
Jesus Christ from the dead...

1 PETER 1:3 NIV

Reflection 26

1 Peter 1:3 Blessed be the God and Father of our Lord
Jesus Christ! According to his great mercy, he has caused
us to be born again to a living hope through the
resurrection of Jesus Christ from the dead,

In 2008 depression set in again even stronger than before.
I tried to handle it by myself, but I couldn't. This time God
sent me professional help and a will to live. I praise him
every day for the precious gift of life. I want to tell you
that the devil is a liar. He should have killed me when I
was of the world. He can't have me now. I also read Psalm
91 on a regular basis and it inspires me more and more
each time I read it. The Psalm tells me just how much God
loves me. I love the Lord and the Lord Loves and smiles on
me. His Love for me makes me smile and for that I am
grateful.

Psalm 91: [5] You will not be afraid of the terror by night,
Or of the arrow that flies by day;
[6] Of the pestilence that [a]stalks in darkness,
Or of the destruction that lays waste at noon.
[7] A thousand may fall at your side
And ten thousand at your right hand, But it shall not
approach you.

Along with using Biblical scriptures, positive affirmations,
what keeps me sane is service. I find that when I show my
gratitude for what God has done for me by helping others I
stay grounded. I believe that helping others is my spiritual
calling, my purpose.

Google's definitions of service is; the action of helping or doing work for someone. I would say that they got it just right.

Professionally, I am a licensed social worker which is a very gratifying profession. What joy it is to see others lives transition from dependence to independence. In my spare time I volunteer for the Center for Dialysis care. For the Center I send out monthly birthday cards. I smile as I sign and address them because I know that the card I send may just be the only one they get. I also volunteer for the Center for Search and Investigation where I post daily on social media notices of missing persons. I've served on multiple ministries at my Church, the most fulfilling one being making visits to patients in nursing homes.

Matthew 25: **42** for I was hungry, and you gave Me *nothing* to eat; I was thirsty, and you gave Me nothing to drink; **43** I was a stranger, and you did not invite Me in; naked, and you did not clothe Me; sick, and in prison, and you did not visit Me.' **44** Then they themselves also will answer, 'Lord, when did we see You hungry, or thirsty, or a stranger, or naked, or sick, or in prison, and did not [e]take care of You?' **45** Then He will answer them, 'Truly I say to you, to the extent that you did not do it to one of the least of these, you did not do it to Me.'

God loves me so I must show love towards others.

PERSONAL REFLECTION:

_____

_____

_____

_____

_____

_____

_____

_____

_____

_____

_____

_____

_____

HARDSHIPS OFTEN PREPARE ORDINARY PEOPLE FOR AN EXTRAORDINARY DESTINY...

-C.S. LEWIS

Reflection 27

2 Corinthians 4:16-18 So we do not lose heart. Though our outer self is wasting away, our inner self is being renewed day by day. For this light momentary affliction is preparing for us an eternal weight of glory beyond all comparison, as we look not to the things that are seen but to the things that are unseen. For the things that are seen are transient, but the things that are unseen are eternal.

It's November 1, 1989; I'm sitting in the dark in the back of the store where I worked and lived. I had finished my last joint, rock of cocaine, and generic beer. I looked around, no one was there, friends were gone, and nothing was left. I began to cry. I felt empty, I felt unnecessary, I felt alone, I felt hopeless, but I didn't feel, do you feel me? I didn't want to live but I was afraid to die.

The prayer that I prayed that turned my life around was only three modest words; GOD HELP ME!! And He did. He heard that simple prayer and started me on the road to life. It was on that day and the result of that that three word prayer that I went from living a life of hopelessness to living a life of purpose. It was on that day that eyes that could not see and ears that could not hear opened up to all the possibilities and promises of God.

It was right then and there that the words of family and friends began to haunt me (in a good way). Their words of hope and encouragement rang out in my head. I knew that I could not live on my own and yes I did want to live. I didn't know what to do, but I did know that there had to be a Power greater than me that could and would change my life.

This day was the beginning of my beginning.

PERSONAL REFLECTION:

_____

_____

_____

_____

_____

_____

_____

_____

_____

_____

Reflection 28

Matthew 6:9 "Pray, then, in this way:' Our Father who is in heaven, Hallowed be Your name. [10] Your kingdom come. Your will be done, On earth as it is in heaven. [11] 'Give us this day our daily bread. [12] 'And forgive us our debts, as we also have forgiven our debtors. [13] 'And do not lead us into temptation, but deliver us from evil. For Yours is the kingdom and the power and the glory forever. Amen.

Not only does God show us His love for us it is also written an example of how we should pray.

It's extremely important to pray, I did not always know that. For so many years I only acknowledged God when I needed someone to blame for the messes that I got myself into.

It was while I was in the mental institution that I realized the importance of prayer. It was in that institution that something amazing happened to me. One night as I prepared for bed, the overwhelming need to pray came over me. I know that it was the wooing of the Holy Spirit because there had only been one other recent time that I had prayed and it was the night when I simply prayed "Help Me". This time I wasn't drunk, I wasn't high.

I was in my room all alone; I did not have a roommate, yes I was alone so I thought. As I was about to get into bed I heard a voice. I looked around expecting to see someone who may have sneaked into the room. There was no one there. Well, no one but me and God. I have to admit that I was somewhat spooked by the voice. I can't describe the voice; all I can say is that it was not mine. The voice told me that I needed to pray.

I fell to my knees which was truly unusual for me. The only times I had been on my knees in over 20 years was when I was desperately searching for any crumb of crack that I could find.

On my knees, I was confused, I didn't know what to do or say. Then I had an ah ha moment, but don't get excited, I was not a positive moment, and I thank God that it was only fleeting. I said to myself (remember, I am in an institution) that God wanted to hear a prayer that was deep, creative, impressive, poetic, a prayer that would have Him come floating down on a ray of sunshine and tell me what a wonderful person I was. NOT!!

PERSONAL REFLECTION:

_____

_____

_____

_____

_____

_____

_____

_____

_____

_____

_____

_____

_____

Now I lay me
Down to sleep, I pray the Lord
My soul to keep,
Angels watch me
Through the night,
And wake me with
The morning light.

Reflection 29

Psalm 3:5 I lay down and slept; I awoke, for the LORD sustains me.

Sanity returned and I am so grateful that it did. In that institution, on my knees, I just wanted to say Thank You. Thank You Lord for saving my life, thank you for giving me a bed to sleep in, three meals a day and people who wanted to be my friend unconditionally. There were people there who talked to me about God, they told me their stories of deliverance, and they told me that there was hope for me.

I was told that I didn't have to live the way I had lived anymore. They provided me with simple steps that I could take to turn my life around. One of those steps was turning my will and live over to the care of God. Why should I turn my will over to Him? Because He loves me more than I could ever love myself.

 Yes, it took being institutionalized for me to come to the realization that I had done things all wrong. My life was in shambles, everything was wrong and I had not been in charge of anything that I had ever taken credit for. I surrendered!

On my knees, I began to cry, I was crying because I could not remember a prayer to pray. I tried to pray the Lord's Prayer but I couldn't remember all of the words. Then out of Heaven words came out of my mouth that amazed me. I look around the room again to see where these words were coming from, I heard my voice but I surely didn't recognize the words right away. Then it came to me, it was my childhood prayer. "Now I lay me down to sleep. I pray the Lord my soul to keep. If I should die before I wake, I pray to God my soul to take. If I should live for other days, I pray the Lord to guide my ways. Amen" Where in the world did that come from? I would never have prayed that childish prayer on my own, I'm 36 years old, I'm grown, or so I thought.

But I got it, I got the message. What God was telling me was that I had to become childlike in order for me to feel His love completely. I had to go back to basics. He need to make me, mold me, bend me, shape me as a potter molds a lump of clay to make it into the beautiful masterpiece that He had always intended it to be.

He is the Potter, I am the clay, I will allow Him to continue molding me into the masterpiece that I know I can be. I'm not quite there yet. I am not who I want to be but I thank God I am not who I used to be. Because He Loves Me.

PERSONAL REFLECTION:

_____

_____

_____

_____

_____

_____

_____

_____

_____

_____

_____

_____

_____

_____

The best decision I ever made was when I looked up to my heavenly father and said, "I cant do this without you. I tried. I failed. I need my God to save me".

Reflection 30

Psalm 120:1 - In my trouble I cried to the LORD, And He answered me.

Despite living through rapes, beatings, overdoses, diseases, homelessness, anger, rage, fear, and despair, I didn't think God was smiling on me. Shame and guilt overwhelmed me day and night. In desperation I wanted to find and know the one and only true God. I went from church to church year after year, not finding what I was looking for. I didn't think God was smiling on me. In February of 2004, it was a Wednesday night. I found Him! Well, I really didn't find Him as He was not lost. I walked into my present Church, The Word Church in Maple Heights OH. There He was, He filled the sanctuary with His Holy Spirit. Glory be to God! I sat and listened, cried, prayed, stood and shouted, praised Him, cried and prayed some more. At last, with no doubt I knew God was smiling on me! I have been through hardships since joining my Church but I know that God Smiles On me. Family problems, financial problems, health problems; but they don't stop me from worshipping the Lord. I know that God smiles on me. I have been taught that delay does not mean denial. I was also taught that when the pupil is ready the teacher will appear.

When down to my lowest even after my deliverance from me, I cried, He heard, He answered. Because He Love Me!

PERSONAL REFLECTION:

_____

_____

_____

_____

_____

_____

_____

_____

_____

_____

_____

_____

_____

_____

ENCOURAGE

ONE ANOTHER

Reflection 31

1 Thessalonians 5:11- Therefore, encourage each other and strengthen one another as you are doing.

It is my sincerest hope and prayer that my story has encouraged someone, anyone to stay the course in spite of your present circumstance. Know that God loves you more that you will ever know.

This book is the first of a series to encourage, empower, motive, and inspire you.
As you have read, I have overcome many obstacles and even when I wanted to give up, my loving God gave me the strength to keep on keeping on.

Depression, self destruction, drugs, alcohol, selfishness, self centeredness, low self esteem, lack of faith or ignorance of faith, suicidal ideations, and desperation consumed me.

How did I overcome? God wouldn't let me quit. Why? Because He loves me and He loves you too.

Today, I am deliberate about my life, I know my purpose and I know that there is a lot more that God has in store for me. I want to be present for my blessings. I shudder at the thought of what I would have missed if I had given up or given in.

Believe me, there are still things that are not to my liking in my life, I cry and ask why me Lord? I ask Him "where are you taking me Lord"? His reply to me is to just keep following Him; I'll know when I get there...

I Won't Quit and neither will you.

PERSONAL REFLECTION:

_____

_____

_____

_____

_____

_____

_____

_____

_____

_____

_____

Don't Quit

When things go wrong, as they sometimes will,
When the road you're trudging seems all uphill,
When the funds are low and the debts are high,
And you want to smile, but you have to sigh,
When care is pressing you down a bit,
Rest, if you must, but don't you quit.

Life is queer with its twists and turns,
As every one of us sometimes learns,
And many a failure turns about,
When he might have won had he stuck it out;
Don't give up though the pace seems slow--
You may succeed with another blow.

Often the goal is nearer than,
It seems to a faint and faltering man,
Often the struggler has given up,
When he might have captured the victor's cup,
And he learned too late when the night slipped down,
How close he was to the golden crown.

Success is failure turned inside out--
The silver tint of the clouds of doubt,
And you never can tell how close you are,
It may be near when it seems so far,
So stick to the fight when you're hardest hit--
It's when things seem worst that you must not quit.

- Author unknown –

PERSONAL REFLECTION:

_____

_____

_____

_____

_____

_____

_____

_____

_____

_____

_____

_____

_____

_____

Notes :

Notes :

Notes :

Notes :

Notes :

Notes :

_____

_____

_____

_____

_____

_____

_____

_____

_____

_____

_____

_____

_____

_____

Notes :

Notes :

Notes :

_____

_____

_____

_____

_____

_____

_____

_____

_____

_____

_____

_____

_____

_____

Notes :

_____

_____

_____

_____

_____

_____

_____

_____

_____

_____

_____

_____

_____

Notes :

Notes :

_____

_____

_____

_____

_____

_____

_____

_____

_____

_____

_____

_____

_____

_____

_____

Notes :

_____

_____

_____

_____

_____

_____

_____

_____

_____

_____

_____

_____

_____

_____

Notes :

Notes :

Notes :

_____

_____

_____

_____

_____

_____

_____

_____

_____

_____

_____

_____

_____

_____

Notes :

_____

_____

_____

_____

_____

_____

_____

_____

_____

_____

_____

_____

Notes :

_____

_____

_____

_____

_____

_____

_____

_____

_____

_____

_____

_____

_____

_____

Notes :

_____

_____

_____

_____

_____

_____

_____

_____

_____

_____

_____

_____

_____

_____

Notes :

_____

_____

_____

_____

_____

_____

_____

_____

_____

_____

_____

_____

_____

Notes :

_____

_____

_____

_____

_____

_____

_____

_____

_____

_____

_____

_____

_____

_____

Notes :

_____

_____

_____

_____

_____

_____

_____

_____

_____

_____

_____

_____

_____

_____

Notes :

Notes :

_____

_____

_____

_____

_____

_____

_____

_____

_____

_____

_____

_____

_____

_____

Notes :

_____

_____

_____

_____

_____

_____

_____

_____

_____

_____

_____

_____

_____

_____

Notes :

_____

_____

_____

_____

_____

_____

_____

_____

_____

_____

_____

_____

_____

_____

Notes :

Notes :

_____

_____

_____

_____

_____

_____

_____

_____

_____

_____

_____

_____

_____

_____

Notes :

_____

_____

_____

_____

_____

_____

_____

_____

_____

_____

_____

_____

_____

_____

_____

Notes :

_____

_____

_____

_____

_____

_____

_____

_____

_____

_____

_____

_____

_____

_____

Notes :

_____

_____

_____

_____

_____

_____

_____

_____

_____

_____

_____

_____

_____

_____

Notes :

_____

_____

_____

_____

_____

_____

_____

_____

_____

_____

_____

_____

_____

_____

Notes :

_____

_____

_____

_____

_____

_____

_____

_____

_____

_____

_____

_____

_____

_____

Notes :

_____

_____

_____

_____

_____

_____

_____

_____

_____

_____

_____

_____

_____

_____

Notes :

_____

_____

_____

_____

_____

_____

_____

_____

_____

_____

_____

_____

_____

Notes :

_____

_____

_____

_____

_____

_____

_____

_____

_____

_____

_____

_____

_____

_____

Notes :

_____

_____

_____

_____

_____

_____

_____

_____

_____

_____

_____

_____

_____

Notes :

Notes :

_____

_____

_____

_____

_____

_____

_____

_____

_____

_____

_____

_____

_____

Notes :

_____

_____

_____

_____

_____

_____

_____

_____

_____

_____

_____

_____

_____

_____

_____

Notes :

_____

_____

_____

_____

_____

_____

_____

_____

_____

_____

_____

_____

_____

About The Author

Tina A. Hobson is the International Best Selling Co-Author of *Success In Beauty: The Secrets to Effortless Fulfillment and Happiness.*

Tina has been in the helping profession for almost 25 years, working as a Licensed Social Worker in the State of Ohio. Ms. Hobson received her BA in Social Work from Capital University in Columbus Ohio. Ms. Hobson has managed many social service programs including those associated with The State of Ohio and Cuyahoga County Alcohol, Drug and Mental Health Services.

Tina speaks publicly and advocates for women's rights including prevention of domestic violence along with sponsoring and hosting Women's Empowerment events. Tina has spoken to thousands, educating on the devastation of addiction to alcohol and other drugs by sharing her personal experience of being delivered from years of using every drug from alcohol to heroin to crack cocaine.

Tina volunteers for The Center for Dialysis Care and The Center for Search and Investigation, helping to find missing children.

Tina is presently the Host of I Am A Superwoman Radio show which is broadcast weekly via Blog Talk Radio and Facebook. The show's goal is To Empower The Superwoman in You!!

She currently sits on the Board of Directors of Man Cry Productions, a local theatrical company, The May Howard Community Project, The Henry Johnson Center and The Proud Women Foundation.

When Tina is not helping others with their personal needs, she manages her own business, Tina's Glory LLC, providing women with the highest quality hair weave along with offering them the opportunity to own their own business and brand their own hair weave. Tina's

Glory LLC is motivated by Scripture in the Holy Bible 1 Corinthians 11:15 "but if a woman has long hair, it is a glory to her? For her hair is given to her for a covering".

Born in Ohio, raised in Chicago, Illinois and Chagrin Falls Ohio, Tina currently resides in Maple Heights Ohio where she works hard at marketing her businesses. Tina believes that with hard work and persistence but first of all having faith in the Provider of All, All Things are Possible. For Speaking and Event Inquiries Contact Heart Centered Women Publishing at 803-414-2117.

One day I met a stranger and that stranger was me, eventually I learned to like her until I came to love me!

www.ingramcontent.com/pod-product-compliance
Lightning Source LLC
Chambersburg PA
CBHW070805100426
42742CB00012B/2255